Contents

CHAPTER 1

Best in show

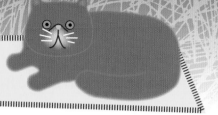

In a busy arena, a crowd gathers around a line of metal cat cages. Inside each cage is a beautiful cat.

It's almost time to compete! Quickly, you give Snowflake, your fluffy white Persian cat, one last brushing. Then you give him a little scratch behind the ears to calm him. Before you know it, a judge is carrying him to a table. You watch nervously as the judge feels Snowflake's face, body, legs and tail. She looks carefully at his ears and eyes. You hope he behaves! Then just as suddenly as it began, it's over. The judge strokes Snowflake and smiles before carrying him back to his cage.

The judge picks up a big blue **rosette**. She carries it to the line of cages and looks carefully at each cat. Then she carries it to Snowflake's cage and pins it to the bars. Everyone around you cheers. Snowflake has been named Best Champion. This award is given to the cat judged the best in its **breed**. Snowflake's first cat show is a success!

rosette ribbon award that is made to look like a rose
breed group of animals within a species that share the same features such as colouring or markings

Did you know?

At most cat shows, rosettes are given as the top prizes. They can be different colours, depending on the show.

BEST OF SHOW

Persians are intelligent, which helps them adjust to being on a judging table.

CHAPTER 2

It's fun to compete

All around the world, from large cities to small towns, people gather to watch beautiful cats compete in shows. Cat shows are judged competitions. Cat owners enter their cats to compete for titles such as Best in Breed or Best in Show. They are exciting events for cat owners, cat breeders and cat lovers alike.

Not all cat shows are the same. Some are small, local and just for fun. Cats at these shows might compete in categories such as "funniest name" or "longest whiskers". Other shows are much larger. National shows attract breeders and owners who are serious about competition. There are even some international cat shows.

A cat remains calm while being judged at a show.

Cat breeding organizations sponsor some of the biggest cat shows. These organizations include The International Cat Association (TICA), the Governing Council of the Cat Fancy and the Cat Fanciers' Association (CFA). One of the biggest cat shows is the CFA's International Cat Show. It's held in a different US city each year.

 ## Costs of competing

Cat show registrations are usually between €30 and €50. Competitors may have to pay other fees for extra grooming space or a cage in a certain spot. They also need to take into account the money they may spend on food, travel and accommodation.

Did you know?

To win the highest award of Grand Champion, a cat needs 200 points. Points are awarded based on wins at cat shows throughout a cat's show career.

Spectators watch as a cat owner prepares for judging.

 ## A big event

Cat shows are busy places. Hundreds of cats of different breeds, ages, colours and genders can compete in a single show. In addition to the cats and their owners, there can be thousands of **spectators**. Adding to the crowd are stalls selling cat toys, collars, beds and treats. In some countries, cat shows are even shown on TV.

People show their cats for different reasons. Some people show **pedigree** or **pure-bred** cats. Performing well at a cat show is a great way for cat breeders to find new customers who might want to buy their kittens. Other people participate in cat shows just for fun. They enjoy meeting other cat owners and seeing the show cats.

Thousands of people attend international competitions.

spectator person who watches an event
pedigree having pure-bred ancestors
pure-bred animal that has been bred from parents and grandparents of the same breed

Championship Class

Cats in this class are eight months old or older, pure-bred and have been **spayed** or **neutered**.

Premier Class or Alter Class

Cats in this class are eight months old or older, pure-bred and have not been spayed or neutered.

Kitten Class

Cats in this class are pure-bred and between four and eight months old.

Veteran Class

Cats competing in this class are pure-bred and older than seven years.

Household Pet Class

Cats competing in this class are mainly non-pedigree or non-pure-bred and have been spayed or neutered. Most competitions require that cats be at least eight months old to compete in this class.

 # Top of the class

Cats competing in shows are divided into different **classes**. These are smaller groups of similar cats that are judged against one another. Depending on the number of competitors, the shows are typically one or two days long. Some common classes at major cat shows include championship, kitten and veteran.

FIRST PLACE

BEST OF COLOR CLASS

Fanci Pantz, a Scottish Fold breed, shows off her ribbons at a cat show in Georgia, USA.

A cat's claws help it to climb.

Claws or no claws?

In some countries many owners choose to declaw their cats. This surgery involves removing the last knuckle and claw from a cat's front paws. Not all shows allow declawed cats to compete. Many people have strong opinions about declawing, and believe it's cruel. They worry that a declawed cat can't defend itself. They also feel that the surgery is painful and unnecessary. Declawing is banned in the UK and many other European countries.

class competition group of cats in a show
spay operate on a female animal so it is unable to produce young
neuter operate on a male animal so it is unable to produce young

Breeds and rules

Cats in shows are often grouped according to their breed. Persian, Siamese and Ragdoll are three common cat breeds. Different cat organizations recognize different numbers of official breeds. For example, TICA recognizes 63 breeds in its championship competitions. It recognizes another 12 in other smaller classes. The CFA recognizes 41 breeds in its championship competitions.

Cats of the same breed compete against one another. The winning cats from each breed then go on to compete in a show's higher levels.

Household cats are judged differently from pure-bred or pedigree cats. Judges score them on qualities such as personality, appearance and uniqueness.

A Sphynx's personality is curious and energetic.

Did you know?

Cat experts believe that the Egyptian Mau is one of the world's oldest cat breeds. These cats were first bred in ancient Egypt.

Bengal cats are the most commonly registered breed with TICA.

Both CFA and TICA record the number of cats registered in each breed. In 2015 the breeds with the most registered cats were:

Cat Fanciers' Association	
1	Exotic
2	Persian
3	Maine Coon
4	Ragdoll
5	British Shorthair

The International Cat Association	
1	Bengal
2	Ragdoll
3	Maine Coon
4	Persian
5	Sphynx

A proud tabby calmly sits at an international cat show in Moscow, Russia.

Prizes

Cat show competitors rarely win money. Instead, they receive different coloured ribbons. At higher levels of competition, the prizes are often large rosettes. The winning cats and their owners also earn recognition. Breeders of winning cats can use these accomplishments to sell kittens to hopeful competitors.

Many people who compete in cat shows say that they are not interested in the awards. They participate because the shows are fun and a way to meet other people with similar interests.

Cat show history

The world's first official cat show was held at London's Crystal Palace in 1871. Artist and writer Harrison Weir organized it. The show was a huge success. Organizers planned a follow-up show later that year.

a portrait of the prize cats drawn by Harrison Weir, the organizer of the first official cat show

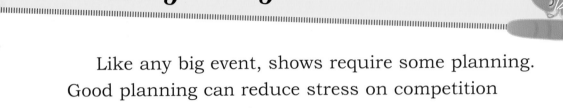

CHAPTER 3

Getting ready for the show

Like any big event, shows require some planning. Good planning can reduce stress on competition day for both you and your cat.

Before entering their cats in a show, cat owners should attend at least one show as spectators. They can see how the competition is organized, how the cats are judged and whether a show would be a good idea for their cats.

Getting the all-clear

Owners also need to take their furry feline friends to the vet for a check-up before shows. Cats must be healthy and have proof that they are up to date with vaccinations before they can enter a competition. Vaccinations help prevent a cat from catching with certain diseases. They help to stop illnesses from spreading to other cats in the competition. Ensuring their cats are vaccinated can also help cat owners to stay healthy.

Cats that will compete in a breed division must often be officially **registered**. Owners who register their cats usually need to provide proof of ancestry along with a small fee to a breed organization.

register enter something on an official list

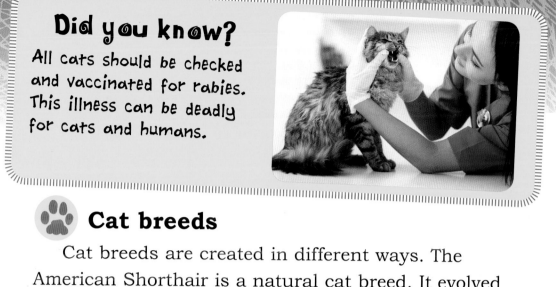
 # Cat breeds

Cat breeds are created in different ways. The American Shorthair is a natural cat breed. It evolved over many generations to be strong, friendly and grow a coat of short fur. Cat owners looking for certain traits created other breeds. Some breeds, such as the Persian and Turkish Angora, are hundreds of years old. Others are quite new. The LaPerm breed began in the United States in the 1980s. Cat breeders liked the cat's unique, curly coat. They bred cats that would pass on this trait.

The LaPerm can have a variety of coats, such as wavy or tight ringlet curls.

Plastic cat carriers can be found at most pet shops or online.

Show supplies

Owners planning to show their cats will need a few supplies before a competition:

- Cat carrier: This large container keeps cats safe during travel. You should always have your cat in a carrier when you travel.

- Carrier cover: These cloth covers fit over the cat carrier. They help to make the cat feel safe and secure inside the carrier. They also help block the cat's view of things that might frighten it, such as dogs or other people.

Grooming tools:

- cat combs and brushes
- facial tissue
- cotton wool and cotton buds
- claw clippers

Different breeds may need different grooming tools. Your vet can recommend the best tools for your cat.

Practice makes perfect

Just like athletes before a big competition, cats need to practise before a show. They need to become comfortable with travel, loud and busy places, and the experience of being judged.

Travel can easily overwhelm a cat. To get their cats used to travel, many show cat owners take their cats on short car journeys. These journeys get cats used to being in their carriers. Some cats are frightened or even become aggressive when they are put in their cat carriers. Practising this task makes travel easier for both a cat and its owner.

Short car journeys allow the owner to practise getting the cat in and out of the carrier.

691

Elegant curtains complement a cat's cage at a show in Birmingham.

Cage curtains

Cage curtains are decorative pieces of cloth owners hang on their cats' cages. Owners often choose cage curtains that complement a cat's colouring or even highlight their cats' personalities. Some are fun and quirky, while others are classical and elegant. Some owners make their own curtains. Others buy them ready-made from speciality pet shops or online.

 ## Dress rehearsal

Owners can also prepare their cats by pretending to be cat show judges. This means placing the cats on tables or worktops and running their hands over the cats' faces, legs, bodies and tails. The owner should look carefully at the cat's ears, eyes and paws. After a cat is comfortable with this process, it's helpful for a friend or family member to pretend to be a judge. This exposes the cat to many people safely handling it.

 ## Cat scratch fever

Cat scratch fever isn't a joke – it's real. And it can be very dangerous. If an infected cat scratches someone, the infection passes through the claws into the person's skin. Humans can also be infected if a cat bite breaks their skin or if a cat licks an open wound on their bodies. Cat scratch fever can make people very sick. That's one good reason to keep your cat's claws clipped.

Did you know?

Cats who scratch or bite a judge or other official are usually disqualified immediately. This rule is for the safety of both the cats and human handlers.

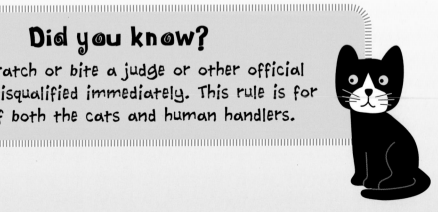

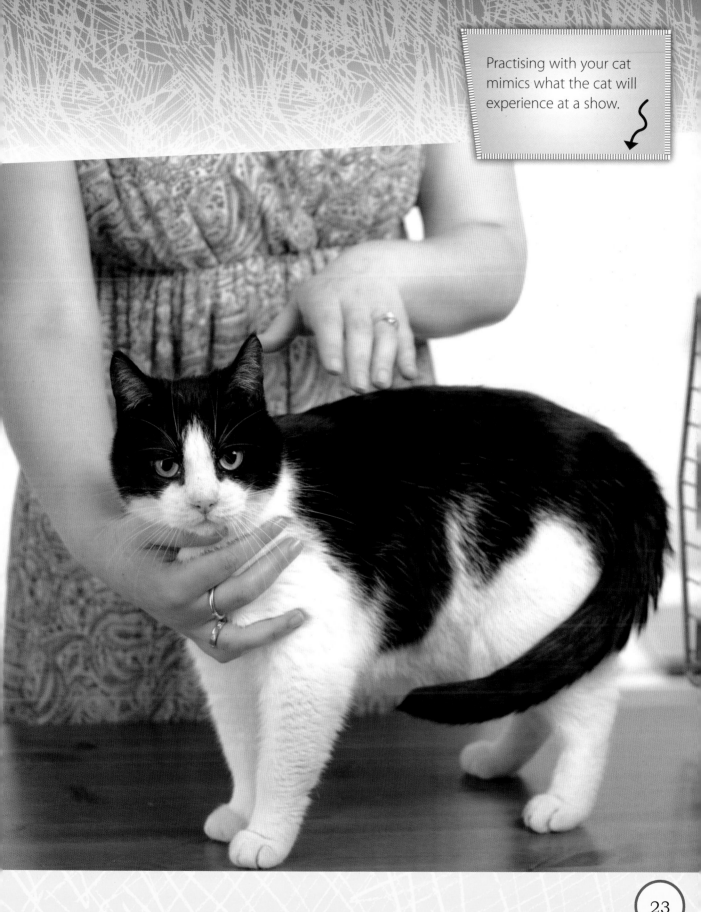

Practising with your cat mimics what the cat will experience at a show.

CHAPTER 4

Show time!

The first morning of a major cat show is busy, exciting and fun. The arena is bustling with owners, cats and cat lovers.

First, competitors check in and receive their cats' cage numbers and show numbers. The cage number tells the owner where to find his or her cat's cage. The cages are typically set up in long lines on display tables. The cage number often includes a row and aisle number. This helps both owners and spectators find cats. The show number is very important. This number is called when it's time for the cat to be judged. At some shows vets examine the cats at check-in as well.

Cat cages are usually plain metal rectangles. Owners add their cats' bedding, food, water and litter tray to the cages to make their cats feel comfortable.

Once they've set up the cages, most cat owners spend the last minutes before judging grooming their cats. This is the time for last-minute touch-ups, such as combing their cats' coats and clipping their claws one last time.

A cat rests in its cage during a competition in Rome, Italy.

Judging

Cat show judges are trained for their jobs. They know the standards for each breed. Standards include traits such as head shape, tail length, colouring and behaviour.

At some shows, owners must leave their cats in a separate judging area. The owners pick up the cats when judging is finished. At other shows, owners can watch the judging along with the spectators.

A judge examines a cat's coat at an international event.

Did you know?

For CFA shows, people who want to become show judges must have at least 10 years of cat breeding experience.

A judge engages with a Sphynx during the Enchanted Cat Club Show in New Mexico, USA.

362

When it is a cat's turn to be judged, a judge or assistant carries it to a judging table. There, the judge strokes the cat, feeling for bone structure, coat quality and build. The judges may take points off the cat's score for flaws or **defects**. These depend on the breed but may include a crooked jaw, crossed eyes or a kink in the cat's tail. The judge also plays with the cat a bit to get a sense of its personality. Judging doesn't take very long. Usually the judge returns the cat to its cage within 30 to 60 seconds.

defect fault or flaw

The final level of competition is often called Best in Show.

 ## The winner!

At most shows, cats earn awards at different levels of competition. During the first level, cats compete within their breed or class. The top-ranked cats then continue to higher levels of competition. The cat of any breed judged to be the very best cat in the competition receives the award of Best in Show.

Cat shows are known for their fun atmosphere and good-natured competition. The next time you hear about a cat show, grab your favourite cat-loving friend and go and take it all in.

How to professionally groom a cat

Even if you won't be taking your cat to a show, you can make your cat look like a winner. If you've never groomed your cat, be very gentle and patient. Over time your cat will look forward to its grooming sessions. Remember that bathing and claw clipping are usually two-person jobs, so ask an adult to help you.

Step 1

Brush your cat's fur with a comb to remove any **mats** or loose hair.

Step 2

Place your cat in a bath or sink with a few centimetres of lukewarm water. Gently wet your cat. Rub cat shampoo into its fur. Rinse the soap from its coat. Gently dry your cat with a towel, and give it a treat as a reward. Many cats don't like being bathed, so be patient. And remember that while your cat should be brushed regularly, it only needs a bath before a show or if it gets too dirty to clean itself.

Step 3

Clip your cat's claws according to your vet's instructions.

Step 4

Once your cat is dry, brush it again. For short-haired cats, use a metal comb and brush from head to tail. For long-haired cats, use a metal comb to brush the cat's body in an upward direction. Be sure to move your brush all the way down to the **underfur**, but don't go down to the skin. If there are any mats in the fur, never try to cut them out yourself. A professional groomer will need to remove these. Finally, part the fur of the tail down the middle. Brush the fur out to each side. When you have detangled the tail, fluff it by brushing it upwards.

Step 5

Using cotton wool and water, wipe out the inside of your cat's ears. Do not put anything into the cat's ear canal.

Step 6

Gently wipe the inner edges of your cat's eyes with moist cotton wool. Wipe in a downward motion.

Step 7

Reward your cat with a treat and a scratch behind the ears.

mat thick, tangled mass of hair
underfur short fur under a long-haired cat's outer coat

Glossary

breed group of animals within a species that share the same features such as colouring or markings

class competition group of cats in a show

defect fault or flaw

mat thick, tangled mass of hair

neuter operate on a male animal so it is unable to produce young

pedigree having pure-bred ancestors

pure-bred animal that has been bred from parents and grandparents of the same breed

register enter something on an official list

rosette ribbon award that is made to look like a rose

spay operate on a female animal so it is unable to produce young

spectator person who watches an event

underfur short fur under a long-haired cat's outer coat

Books

Animal Classification: Do Cats Have Family Trees? (Show Me Science) Eve Hartman and Wendy Meshbesher (Raintree, 2014)

Caring for Cats and Kittens (Battersea Dogs & Cats Home Pet Care Guides), Ben Hubbard (Franklin Watts, 2015)

The Cat Encyclopedia (DK Cats), DK (Dorling Kindersley, 2014)

The Complete Cat Breed Book, DK (Dorling Kindersley, 2013)

 Websites

www.cats.org.uk/cat-care/cats-for-kids

Find out some fascinating feline facts, take part in fun activities and games and get useful cat care advice.

www.rspca.org.uk/adviceandwelfare/pets/cats

Find out more about cat behaviour.

Comprehension questions

1. What are some of the things you need to take with you to a cat show? What are they used for?

2. What are some things a judge looks for when interacting with a cat? What are some of the things that can earn a cat points?

3. On pages 4–5, a cat is about to be awarded the Best Champion rosette. Imagine that you are that cat. What are you feeling? Write a short diary entry about your experiences at the cat show.

Index